WEAPONS AND WARFARE

WEAPONS AND WARFARE

ADRIAN GILBERT

FRANKLIN WATTS

LONDON • SYDNEY

Designer Thomas Keenes
Editor Sarah Ridley
Art Director Jonathan Hair
Editor-in-Chief John C. Miles
Picture Research Diana Morris

First published in 2004
by Franklin Watts
96 Leonard Street
London
EC2A 4XD

Franklin Watts Australia
45-51 Huntley Street
Alexandria
NSW 2015

ISBN 0 7496 5150 4

A CIP catalogue record for this book
is available from the British Library.

Printed in Malaysia

Picture credits
IWM/TRH: 15b, 23c, 25b
Peter Newark's Pictures: front and
back cover background, 2, 7, 8-9,
10b, 11t, 17t, 19, 20c, 21b, 27b
Popperfoto: 13t
Topham Picturepoint: 16b, 29

*Every attempt has been made to clear
copyright. Should there be any inadvertent
omission, please apply to the publisher for
rectification.*

Artwork
Mark Bergin, Peter Visscher, Mike
White

CONTENTS

A WORLD AT WAR

The assassination of Archduke Francis Ferdinand in Sarajevo pushed Europe into a war that spread around the globe. Millions were killed in four years of brutal fighting. At the end of the war new countries were created leaving four empires in ruins.

COMPLEX BACKGROUND

The reasons why an assassination led to world war were many and complex. At the heart of the problem was the attitude of Germany and the alliance system that divided Europe into two armed camps, each afraid of the other.

Germany was the major industrial and military power in Europe but resented the large colonial empires of France and Britain and their influence in Europe. France, meanwhile, afraid that it might be attacked by Germany, allied itself with Russia for protection. Although Britain did not join an alliance, it supported France and Russia against Germany. When the German army marched through Belgium in 1914, Britain declared war on Germany.

DOMINO EFFECT

Germany's only major ally was Austria-Hungary, which was engaged in a long-running dispute with the small nation-state of Serbia, which was supported by Russia. When Austria-Hungary put pressure on Serbia after the assassination of Francis Ferdinand, Russia made it clear that it would come to Serbia's aid. More countries were sucked into the war as time passed: Turkey and Bulgaria joined the Central Powers; Italy, Portugal and the United States joined in on the side of the Allies.

GRINDING DOWN THE ENEMY

Over the course of the war, the superior economic and military strength of the Allies wore down the Central Powers, so that in November 1918 they were forced to

---

KAISER WILHELM II

A GRANDSON OF QUEEN VICTORIA, Kaiser Wilhelm II (1859-1941) came to the German throne in 1888 and encouraged Germany to adopt an aggressive foreign policy. He helped supervise the dramatic expansion of the German navy, which brought Germany into growing conflict with Britain. Wilhelm also supported the Austro-Hungarian clash with Serbia, and this led to the outbreak of World War One.

When Germany faced defeat in 1918, Wilhelm was forced to abdicate and spent the rest of his life in exile in the Netherlands.

RAILWAY FOR WAR

The generals on all sides were obsessed with getting as many troops as possible to the battlefield – and as quickly as possible. In 1914 the entire German military plan depended on their troops following a fixed railway timetable. Seven German armies, totalling 1,485,000 men, would quickly advance by rail to the French borders and then defeat France.

An idealised view of a British soldier saying goodbye and going off to war.

1914: Countdown To War

28 June	Assassination of Archduke Francis Ferdinand.
6 July	Germany promises support for Austria-Hungary.
28 July	Austria-Hungary declares war on Serbia.
30 July	Russia begins to mobilise (prepare for war).
1 August	Germany declares war on Russia.
3 August	Germany declares war on France.
4 August	Germany declares war on Belgium.
4 August	Britain declares war on Germany.
6 August	Austria-Hungary declares war on Russia.

☞ WORLD WAR ONE

◆ Archduke Francis Ferdinand, the heir to the Austro-Hungarian throne, and his wife were killed in the Bosnian city of Sarajevo by nationalists operating from Serbia.

◆ Before 1914, the main task of German commanders was to prepare plans for the next war. Having decided that Russia and France were Germany's most likely enemies, their plan was to launch an offensive against France in the west and then turn eastwards and attack Russia.

◆ Germany and Austria-Hungary (and later Turkey and Bulgaria) were called the Central Powers, while France, Russia, Britain and its empire and Belgium (and later Italy, Portugal and the United States) were called the Allies.

◆ Approximately 13 million people were killed in World War One, most of them young men.

accept the Allied peace terms (armistice). Revolution – sparked off primarily by the war – brought an end to the Russian Empire in 1917, while the empires of Germany and Austria-Hungary collapsed in 1918. The Ottoman (Turkish) Empire also fell apart at the end of the war, and lost many of its pre-war territories.

INDUSTRY AND WARFARE

World War One was the first major European conflict for nearly a century. During that time, the technological advances made possible by the Industrial Revolution had a profound impact on warfare.

INDUSTRIAL REVOLUTION

The dramatic increase in economic output and technological progress that we call the Industrial Revolution began in Britain in the late 18th century and then spread to Europe and the United States. The Industrial Revolution changed almost every aspect of the way people lived and worked – and it also had an enormous impact on the way that war was waged.

During the 19th century, improvements in living conditions encouraged a dramatic increase in the population of Europe. This, in turn, led to the creation of much bigger armies. In addition, because countries

ALFRED KRUPP

A STEEL AND ARMAMENTS manufacturer, Alfred Krupp (1812-87) played a major role in making Germany an economic and military power in the 19th century.

Krupp manufactured the first all-steel gun in 1847. The Krupp Company was quick to adopt the newly developed Bessemer steelmaking process and other new metalworking techniques. As a result, its artillery was the most advanced and accurate in the world.

As well as arms and steel production, Krupp acquired mines and collieries that made the Ruhr region of western Germany the most powerful industrial centre in Europe.

A gun-finishing shop at the Krupps factory in Essen, Germany, in about 1900.

were now much richer, they could afford to keep large numbers of men away from their normal jobs for longer periods of time than before.

YEAR-ROUND RATIONS

The widespread introduction of canned food in the late 19th century enabled armies to fight throughout the year. In the past, armies normally retired from the battlefront to winter quarters because of shortages of food.

MORE POWERFUL WEAPONRY

Another major consequence of the Industrial Revolution lay in the increased power of weapons: they had a much greater range, were more accurate and more destructive. And as well as the improvements to existing weapons, such as rifles and artillery, technological development led to the invention of new weapons, which by 1914 included the machine-gun.

The combination of new technology, increased size of the armies and the determination of politicians and generals to win at any cost ensured that casualties would be extremely heavy.

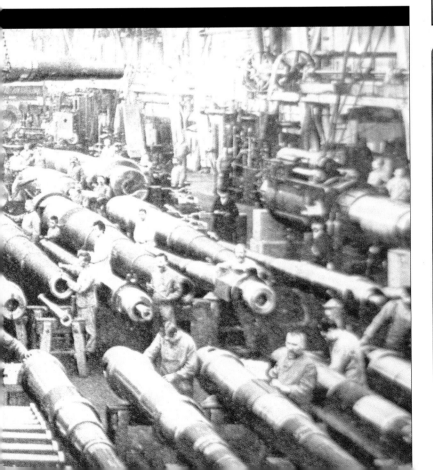

Industrial Developments

1856 Invention of the Bessemer converter, enabling steel to be produced cheaply and in large quantities.

1867 Development of the first electric dynamo by the German company, Siemens.

1867 Invention of dynamite, a stable but very powerful explosive, by Swedish-born inventor Alfred Nobel.

1876 Invention of the telephone by Scottish-born Canadian, Alexander Graham Bell.

1879 Invention of the electric lamp by American inventor, Thomas Edison.

1885 Development of an effective internal-combustion engine, used to power a small three-wheeled car, by German engineer Karl Benz.

1900 Transmission of the first radio message across the Atlantic by Italian-born inventor, Guglielmo Marconi.

1903 Successful flight in the first powered and controllable aircraft is achieved by two American brothers, the inventors Wilbur and Orville Wright.

☛ TECHNOLOGY

◆ Steel production was considered a useful guide to the economic strength of a country. In Europe, Germany was clearly the leader in 1914, producing 17 million tonnes of steel a year. Britain came second with just under seven million tonnes, then France and Russia, both with a little over four million tonnes.

◆ Britain was the world's leading trading nation. In 1866 it possessed six million tonnes of merchant shipping; by 1914 the figure had risen to 21 million tonnes.

◆ Aviation developed rapidly in the early 1900s, with France taking the lead. In 1909 Louis Blériot flew across the English Channel.

1914: WEAPONS OF WAR

Soldiers going to war in August 1914 had hopes that the fighting would be over "by Christmas", but they were wrong. In France and Belgium, the destructive power of weaponry forced armies into a line of defensive trenches – known as the "Western Front" – for the next four years.

RIFLES, MACHINE-GUNS AND FIELD ARTILLERY

All the different armies of 1914 went to war with similar weapons. The most important were rifles, machine-guns and field guns.

During the 19th century the rifle had been steadily improved, and by 1914 it was both fast-firing and accurate. Snipers and other marksmen could hit a man at a distance of 1,000 metres in good conditions. Ordinary, well-trained infantry would hold their fire until the enemy was about 550 metres away. At this range, well-trained troops created a "beaten-zone", so that the majority of troops advancing into this zone would be killed or wounded, almost certainly bringing any attack to a halt.

"The war has got stuck into a gigantic siege on both sides. The whole front is one endless fortified trench."

Captain Rudolph Binding,
a German officer, describes conditions on
the Western Front, November 1914

A battery of French 75-mm field guns, capable of rapid and accurate fire.

A German machine-gun crew dug in on the Western Front.

THE INTRODUCTION OF THE MACHINE-GUN

The power of static defence over mobile attack was increased by the introduction of machine-guns. Of these, the water-cooled Maxim-type guns used by Germany, Britain and Russia were the most effective. A machine-gun crew of just two men could fire up to 600 bullets per minute, and although machine-guns fired standard rifle bullets they had an effective range of more than 1,000 metres.

FIELD ARTILLERY

The third main weapon used by the armies of 1914 was field artillery. This came in two types: field guns and field howitzers. Field guns, such as the French "75" and the British 18-pounder, fired a high-velocity shrapnel shell (see right) directly towards the target. Field howitzers, such as the British 4.5-inch and the Austro-Hungarian 149-mm "Modell 14", lobbed an explosive shell in a high arc towards the enemy.

The sheer power of modern weapons made warfare in the open impossible. The French had originally encouraged their troops to attack at all costs and as a result suffered approximately one million casualties in the war's opening battles. Soldiers now had to fight under cover, and this led to the construction of a trench system. By the end of 1914, trenches stretched from the North Sea all the way to the Alps.

SIR HIRAM MAXIM

BORN IN THE UNITED STATES, Hiram Maxim (1840-1916) was an engineer and inventor who began his career developing different types of gas and electric lights. He later moved to Britain, where he perfected his recoil-action machine-gun in 1883. The British army took an interest and, after modifications, it was manufactured as the Vickers machine-gun.

German and Russian armies also realised the effectiveness of Maxim's invention and armed their own soldiers with a similar weapon. Maxim, who became a British citizen, was knighted in 1901.

◆ KIT AND GUNS

◆ The infantrymen of 1914 were heavily weighed down by their equipment, rifles and ammunition (easily weighing 30 kg), yet they were expected to march long distances – up to 30 kilometres a day.

◆ British riflemen were so skilled that, by 1914, they were able to fire up to 25 aimed shots per minute. This was so fast that the Germans thought they were armed with machine-guns.

◆ The French army's 75-mm field gun was the best light artillery piece in the world in 1914. It had a range of 11,000 metres and, because of its revolutionary recoil system, it had a very high rate of fire – more than 20 rounds per minute for extended time periods.

◆ Shrapnel was an artillery shell used against troops in the open. It contained hundreds of steel balls and was designed to explode in the air, so that the contents blasted down on the enemy soldiers below.

NAVAL NATIONS

Britain and Germany were the two major naval powers of World War One. Both nations had built up large fleets dominated by "dreadnoughts" - a new type of heavily armoured and formidably gunned battleship.

A NEW BATTLESHIP

HMS *Dreadnought* was launched in 1906. It was a revolutionary vessel that made all other battleships obsolete overnight. *Dreadnought* was faster, better armed and had heavier armour protection than any other battleship afloat at the time. The key to its success lay in two features. It had steam-turbine engines, which gave it a long range and a top speed of 21 knots. It also had an "all-big-gun" armament of 10 12-inch guns in five armoured turrets. These guns were capable of hitting enemy ships at ranges of up to 20,000 metres.

After the launch of HMS *Dreadnought*, all other modern battleships followed a similar pattern, so that they became known as dreadnoughts. Britain and Germany raced to build as many as possible, but Britain had a head start. By the end of the war it had 48 dreadnoughts against Germany's 26.

DESTROYERS – FAST AND LIGHT

Despite the awesome power of the dreadnought battleship, it was considered vulnerable to the torpedo,

> *"Confused, with one or two momentary exceptions of paralysing terror, own gunfire and enemy's flashes and a hail of splinters."*

A British officer describes his impressions of the Battle of Jutland

Naval Chronology

1894 Launch of *Turbinia*, the world's first turbine-propelled vessel, capable of a speed of 30 knots.

1906 Launch of HMS *Dreadnought* – the first of the all-big-gun, turbine-powered ships that was to transform battleship design.

1914, 22 September The sinking of three British cruisers in succession by the German U-boat (submarine) U-9 provides a "wake-up call" for Britain to the threat from submarines.

1916, 31 May The Battle of Jutland is fought between the main British and German fleets. The Germans sink more British ships but are forced back into harbour.

ADMIRAL JOHN FISHER

JOHN FISHER (1841-1920) was a naval reformer who played a key role in modernising Britain's Royal Navy in the years leading up to World War One. He encouraged improvements in naval gunnery and was the guiding force behind the introduction of the dreadnought.

Fisher was one of the few senior naval officers who realised that the submarine would be a threat in any future war. He also tried to break down the class system in the Royal Navy to allow able officers from any background to rise to senior rank.

A view between two huge gun turrets of a church service on board HMS *Queen Elizabeth* in the Dardanelles in 1915.

which was fired from fast torpedo boats and submarines. To protect the main fleet of battleships, a special class of fast, light ships, called destroyers, was developed. Capable of speeds of at least 30 knots, they were also armed with torpedoes so that they could attack enemy battleships as well as defend them from smaller ships.

SCOUTING OUT THE ENEMY

The other main type of surface warship was the cruiser, which was somewhere between the battleship and the destroyer in the size and power of its guns. There were many different types of cruiser but their chief function was to "cruise" independently of the main battle fleet, acting as scouts to find the enemy, attacking merchant ships and smaller types of naval vessel.

NAVAL TECHNOLOGY

◆ Designed by the British engineer Sir Charles Parsons, the steam turbine was a more efficient way of delivering power to a ship's propellers than older types of marine steam engine.

◆ Parsons concocted a brilliant sales demonstration in 1897 when his launch *Turbinia* zipped between slower ships in front of a huge crowd watching Queen Victoria's Diamond Jubilee Naval Review at Spithead.

◆ A marine turbine rotating at high speed creates a lot of stress and Parsons was only able to develop the turbine in the 1890s because super-strong steels became available.

◆ The Royal Navy began to change over from coal to oil power in the early 1900s because oil was more efficient than coal and did not produce as much smoke.

◆ The five British *Queen Elizabeth*-class battleships were the most advanced of World War One. They had a top speed of 25 knots and were armed with eight 15-inch guns.

THE ENEMY BELOW

The submarine was originally designed to attack warships. However, its most effective role was to cripple an enemy by sinking its merchant shipping, thereby cutting off vital supplies. German U-boats (submarines) almost managed to starve Britain into surrender in 1917.

MENACE UNDER THE WATER

Although in many ways marvels of technology, the submarines of World War One had a limited fighting ability when underwater. Once submerged, they relied on electric motors. These were slow, however, and had a restricted range before the batteries, which supplied them with power, had to be recharged.

Submarines spent most of their time sailing on the surface using their gun-power to sink enemy merchant ships, and only submerging when enemy warships were close by. Most submarines carried only a few torpedoes – typically between four and six. These were only fired when surface action was too dangerous.

U-BOATS WREAK HAVOC

Despite these limitations, German U-boats played a deadly role in the war against Britain, sinking vast numbers of ships sailing to and from British ports. In February 1917 the Germans launched an all-out submarine offensive, attacking all ships in British waters. By the end of June nearly three million tonnes of shipping had been sunk, and ships from neutral countries were avoiding British ports. Only a six-week supply of corn remained in the country when British naval officers admitted they had lost control of the sea. The U-boats were winning the war.

U-boats were ultimately defeated by the introduction of new tactics and weapons. At the end of April 1917 the British began to group all their merchant ships

> *"The submarine is the most formidable thing the war has produced."*
>
> Walter Page, US ambassador to London

JP HOLLAND

THE INVENTOR of the modern submarine was Irish-born American John Philip Holland (1840-1914). After many failed attempts, he successfully launched his vessel *Holland VI* in 1898.

This boat cleverly managed to combine a number of mainly new technologies. It was powered by an internal-combustion engine on the surface and an electric motor while submerged. It had hydroplanes and ballast tanks to regulate underwater travel, and was fitted with a periscope and torpedo tubes. *Holland VI* was the basic design behind all naval submarines of World War One.

together into convoys, which were protected by naval vessels armed with anti-submarine weapons.

DETECTING U-BOATS

One of the major problems for the British was locating U-boats when underwater. Hydrophones, which detected the sound of a submarine's propellers underwater, were a useful but limited aid. In reality, the captain of the anti-submarine ship had to use his experience to guess where the U-boat might be. Depth charges – powerful explosives that detonated at pre-set depths – were effective when U-boats were discovered.

Other weapons and tactics employed against U-boats included the use of sea mines and ramming by fast convoy escort vessels – a total of 19 U-boats were destroyed by ramming. By early 1918 the number of U-boats sunk was rising and the number of merchant ships sunk was falling. The tide of the war had turned.

U-BOATS

◆ The German U-35 was the most successful submarine of World War One. It sank 224 vessels; a total of 535,900 tonnes of shipping.

◆ Launched at the end of the war, the German U-139 class were enormous ocean-going submarines, armed with two 150-mm guns and 19 torpedoes. They could stay at sea for several months and had a range of 23,150 kilometres.

◆ By the end of the war, Germany had deployed 372 U-boats; 192 were sunk. A total of 5,409 crewmen were killed – more than half the total of men who served in U-boats.

◆ Torpedoes had a maximum range of around 9,000 metres and a speed of 28 knots by 1914.

German submarine U-35 on the surface in the Mediterranean, showing the conning tower.

BIG GUNS

Artillery was the single most important weapon of the war; more soldiers were killed or wounded by it than by any other weapon. Its destructive power created the shell-pocked landscape of the Western Front.

DEFENDING AND ATTACKING

Artillery was employed as both a defensive and offensive weapon. In defence, artillery was used to halt enemy attacks by killing troops advancing across no-man's-land and by breaking up reserve formations waiting just behind the frontline trenches. The enemy's own guns were also attacked, in what was known as counter-battery fire.

"CREEPING BARRAGE"

In attack, artillery destroyed the enemy's frontline trenches, knocked out enemy guns (counter-battery fire) and provided a "creeping barrage" to protect its own infantry. A creeping barrage consisted of guns firing their shells in a line just

A British officer and an Armenian artilleryman fire a Russian 6-inch howitzer in the Middle East, August 1918.

A massive German railway gun in position with its camouflage net.

ahead of the advancing infantry. As the infantry moved forward, the barrage would "creep" forward as well.

The number of guns increased steadily through the war. At the Battle of the Somme in 1916 the British had just over 2,000 guns. For their Spring Offensive of 1918 the Germans had more than three times that number.

UNABLE TO ATTACK

Although artillery was the war's key weapon it caused a major problem for troops trying to attack. The massive bombardments churned up the ground so much that infantry found it difficult to advance across what had become a mass of shell craters. Wheeled vehicles, including artillery, found the frontline area impassable. As a result, attacks soon ground to a halt, allowing the defenders time to bring up reserves and build new lines of trenches.

"I lost all count of the shells and all count of time. There was not past or future. Only the present. The present agony of waiting, waiting for the shell that was coming to destroy us, waiting to die."

A British soldier describes a German artillery bombardment

COLONEL GEORG BRUCHMÜLLER

A GERMAN ARTILLERYMAN, Georg Bruchmüller (1863-1948) was a pioneer of advanced artillery tactics. Early in the war, most bombardments lasted days, sometimes weeks. Bruchmüller, however, aimed to employ the element of surprise.

By 1916 he had adopted short, heavy bombardments, which would last just a few hours. His belief was that this was enough to knock out strong points rather than attempt to destroy the entire enemy position.

Bruchmüller was very successful in organising the intense and complex artillery barrage against the British in the German Spring Offensive of 1918.

☛ ARTILLERY

◆ Most field guns had a range of between 7,000-11,000 metres, while the majority of heavier guns operated at ranges of between 10,000-20,000 metres.

◆ In order to destroy the many forts that defended Belgium in 1914, the Germans developed a special 420-mm howitzer that could smash through thick concrete. The gun was large and squat, and German troops nicknamed it "Big Bertha" after the granddaughter of Alfred Krupp.

◆ The French 520-mm Schneider howitzer had a range of over 19,000 metres and fired the heaviest shell used in the war. At 1,425 kilograms, the shell was roughly the weight of a large family car today.

◆ More than three million shells were fired in the opening artillery barrage of the huge German Spring Offensive of March 1918.

SCOUTS AND FIGHTERS

The introduction of aircraft transformed warfare. The first aircraft were used solely for reconnaissance but they soon developed into deadly fighting machines.

LOCATING INFORMATION

In 1914 military aircraft were flimsy machines that carried no guns. A few intrepid pilots armed themselves with revolvers and rifles, however, and took pot shots at any enemy aircraft they saw. The role of these early flying machines was to use their height and range to locate enemy gun batteries and spot new trenches and the movement of troops. This intelligence could have dramatic results: on 2 September 1914 a keen-eyed French aviator reported the major change in the German advance that led to the invasion of France being halted at the First Battle of the Marne.

Until 1915, senior commanders had to rely on verbal reports and simple sketches from the aircrew. But the introduction of aerial photography provided them with a detailed visual description of what lay beyond the enemy front line. Throughout the war, reconnaissance remained the key function of all air forces.

"SPY IN THE SKY"

The next step was to destroy the enemy reconnaissance aircraft, the "spy in the sky". Anti-aircraft guns were used in large numbers but were not very effective. The best technique was to send another aircraft to shoot it down. Once interrupter gear had been developed in 1915, to allow the forward firing of a machine-gun through a whirling propeller, the true fighter aircraft emerged. It was fast, manoeuvrable and deadly.

The fighter aircraft produced a new breed of pilots. Known as "aces", they were skilful and ruthless in equal measure. Only a few of them survived the war but the best of them acquired impressive scores of enemy aircraft they had shot down.

> *"Oh, it was a good fight, and the Huns [Germans] were fine sports. One tried to ram me, after he was hit, and only missed me by inches."*

British fighter ace Captain Albert Ball (shot down and killed in 1917)

ANTHONY FOKKER

Born in Holland, Anthony Fokker (1890-1939) opened an aircraft factory in Germany in 1913, and there he manufactured military aircraft for the German armed forces throughout the war. He was an exceptionally talented designer. As well as inventing the first effective interrupter gear, he also built some of the best fighter aircraft of the war, including the Fokker triplane flown by Baron Manfred von Richthofen, popularly known as the "Red Baron".

After the war he returned to Holland and then moved to the United States.

A British squadron of SE5a aircraft lined up on their airfield in France, 1918.

◆ The first great fighter pilots of the war were the two German aces, Max Immelmann and Oswald Boelcke. They achieved fame with Fokker fighters in 1915, although both were killed in the following year.

◆ Fighter pilots who shot down five (or, in the German air force, ten) enemy aircraft were known as "aces". The top aces of the war were Manfred von Richthofen (German, 80 kills), René Fonck (French, 75 kills), Edward "Mick" Mannock (British, 73 kills) and William "Billy" Bishop (Canadian, 72 kills).

◆ Air forces increased massively in size throughout the war. By November 1918 the British Royal Air Force had 22,500 aircraft and nearly 300,000 men under its command.

◆ The British SE5a fighter shot down more German aircraft than any other Allied warplane.

FIRING THROUGH THE PROPELLER

For an aircraft to become an effective fighter, its machine-guns had to be able to fire along the line of the fuselage – but the propeller got in the way. The first solution to this problem was to fit angled steel plates on the two propeller blades so the bullets would be deflected.

Anthony Fokker developed a much better solution in August 1915. He fitted an interrupter gear, which briefly stopped the machine-gun when the propeller blade swung into the path of each bullet. Until the Allies developed their own interrupter system, the Germans possessed a great advantage in aerial combat.

TRENCH WARFARE

Trench warfare dominated the Western Front for four years. During this time, new weapons came into being as a direct result of the experience of war in the trenches.

TRENCH STRUCTURE

The frontline trenches of each side were heavily fortified with sandbags and barbed wire. They were separated by a stretch of ground called no-man's-land, which was between 50 and 500 metres wide. Behind the frontline trench was a series of at least two support trenches. These trenches were connected by communication trenches, which allowed men and supplies to move reasonably safely in and out of the main trenches.

Machine-guns were positioned in key points along the trench system, while artillery was sited in gun pits some distance behind. Field and medium guns were positioned near the trenches and heavy guns were set up between 2,000 and 4,000 metres behind the front line.

RE-INVENTION OF A DEADLY WEAPON

Among the first of the new trench weapons was a re-invention of a late 17th-century device, the grenade. Although they had a short range – only as far as a man

A German sentry waits with a stick grenade and watches the enemy through a camouflaged trench periscope in 1916.

> *"The ground began to rock. In front the earth opened and a large mass mounted on pillars of fire rose to the sky, where it seemed to remain suspended for some seconds while the awful red glow lit up the surrounding desolation."*

A British soldier describes explosive mines being detonated on Messines Ridge, 1917

WAR UNDERGROUND

Rather than continuing to pound enemy trenches with artillery, each side also dug tunnels underneath the enemy's trenches, packing them with explosives and then blowing them up just before a major attack.

The most devastating instance of military mining took place in 1917, when the British dug 21 mines under Messines Ridge, filling each mine with about 9,000 kilograms of explosives. When they were detonated on 7 June, the explosion annihilated the German forward positions, allowing the attacking troops to occupy their trenches with few casualties.

could throw – the grenade's combination of high explosive and steel splinters was deadly in the confined spaces of the trenches.

Another older weapon to be re-used in the trenches was the mortar. The mortar of 1914-18 normally consisted of a simple steel tube that lobbed a high-explosive shell into the opposite trench. Introduced in 1915, mortars became increasingly numerous, and with increased accuracy and range – up to 1,500 metres – they were known as the "infantryman's artillery".

RAIDING PARTIES

Raids were another tactic used in trench warfare. These usually took the form of night attacks made by small groups of men to capture prisoners. In order to be as quiet as possible, the raiders were often armed simply with hand-made clubs and bayonets and daggers. Such weapons proved surprisingly effective in hand-to-hand fighting.

◗ TRENCH WARFARE

◆ Snipers were marksmen armed with highly accurate rifles fitted with telescopic sights. Their precise fire forced the enemy to keep their heads down. They caused heavy casualties when soldiers were careless.

◆ Reinforced-concrete blockhouses developed by the Germans in 1917 were nicknamed "pill boxes" by the British, who thought they looked like the cardboard pill containers in use at the time.

◆ Steel helmets were introduced by the French, German and British armies during 1915-16 to protect troops from the effect of shell splinters. Soldiers have worn similar helmets ever since.

◆ The explosions under Messines Ridge were so loud they were heard more than 220 kilometres away in London.

◆ In order to increase the range of grenades, special cartridges were developed that allowed them to be fired from the end of rifles. Although not very accurate, rifle grenades could be fired over 200 metres.

German stormtroops train at Sedan in May 1917, on shell-pocked ground. They carry bags of grenades slung around their necks.

SUPPORT SERVICES

In order to ensure that the vast armies of World War One could carry on fighting, they had to be supplied with food, weapons and equipment on a massive scale. The supply of the frontline troops, known as logistics, called for high levels of organisational skill.

DELIVERING SUPPLIES

On the Western Front huge depots were set up behind the front line, and every day millions of tonnes of stores would be sent up to the trenches. Railways provided the key to this logistical system. On the Western Front, there was already a well developed rail system, and this was used extensively by all the armies. In addition, thousands of kilometres of light railway were built to take heavy equipment, especially ammunition for the artillery, up to the front.

"Once troops were committed to the attack, all control was lost."

A British officer describes the difficulties of commanding troops during an offensive

COMMUNICATION PROBLEMS

A major problem for generals was to keep in contact with troops spread out over large areas. The telephone was the main method of sending orders and receiving information. During a battle, however, the telephone lines were often cut by artillery fire.

Once the troops had left their frontline trenches, senior officers often had little idea what was going on in the battle. The solution to this problem was radio – or "wireless" – but in World War One radios were very bulky and did not work well.

HORSEPOWER

Motor transport increased dramatically as the war progressed. In 1914 the British army had 1,485 motor vehicles. By 1918 this had expanded to a figure of 121,700. And yet despite this vast increase, the horse remained the chief carrier of men and supplies. Even in 1918, a British infantry division was equipped with 822 horse-drawn vehicles (and a grand total of over 8,000 horses) as against fewer than 40 motor vehicles. And like their human counterparts, horses had a voracious appetite for food.

Despite the size of the armies, the supply systems of

British motor lorries at Cambrai wait to be loaded with artillery shells in 1918.

both sides generally worked well. British troops were better supplied than most. Even in the worst weather and during offensives, the ordinary British soldier rarely went without adequate supplies of food. And to maintain the men's morale an excellent postal system was introduced so that soldiers could receive and send letters from the front line in a matter of days. Although the Allied commanders have been criticised for the heavy casualties suffered by their troops, they went to great trouble to see that the men were well looked after.

SUPPLY LINES

◆ In 1914 the German First Army – the biggest of the seven armies that attacked France – was equipped with 84,000 horses. They consumed 900 tonnes of fodder every day.

◆ Each German division was assigned 20 "message" dogs and five handlers for communication when telephone lines were destroyed. Pigeons were also used to send messages.

◆ Simple radios were fitted to aircraft to help improve the accuracy of artillery. The observer or pilot would send Morse-code messages to tell the artillery officer on the ground if the gun's shells were hitting or missing their targets, and correct them if they were not.

◆ Most British troops received a daily rum ration, which proved very popular. But in certain units senior officers disapproved of alcohol so the men were given other "treats", such as pea soup, which were far less popular!

AIR ATTACK

World War One witnessed the emergence of a new way of waging war – the attack of targets deep behind enemy lines by bomber aircraft. Civilians as well as soldiers were now vulnerable to assaults from the skies.

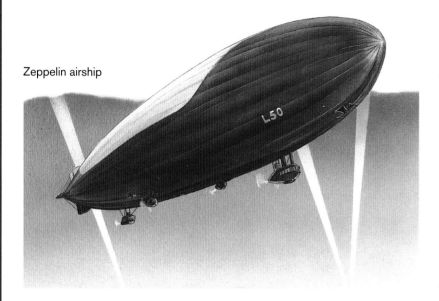
Zeppelin airship

"It was not easy to believe that these little silver specks far up in the heavens had the power to bring death and destruction."

An American journalist describes the beginning of the German air raid on London on 13 June 1917

BASIC BOMBING

The first attempts at bombing were very basic and involved throwing home-made explosives out of the cockpit. By 1915, however, a true bomber had evolved with bombs carried under the fuselage and bomb-aiming sights.

Attacks on and just behind the enemy front line came to be called tactical bombing. This involved direct, short-range sorties (flights) on military targets by single-engined aircraft. By the end of the war, tactical bombing led to the emergence of the ground-attack aircraft. This was fitted with armour plating under the fuel tank and pilot's cockpit for protection against machine-gun and rifle fire from ground troops.

NOWHERE IS SAFE

The other major type of aerial assault was called strategic bombing, which were raids against economic and civilian targets. The first strategic bombing raids came with the German zeppelin airship attacks against

GENERAL FERDINAND VON ZEPPELIN

A GERMAN SOLDIER, General Ferdinand von Zeppelin (1838-1917) retired from the army in 1891 to pursue his interest in airships. His first successful airship flew in 1900, and was constructed using a rigid frame over which was stretched a tightly sealed covering. It was then inflated with hydrogen. Once war was declared, his airships, called zeppelins, were mainly used for naval reconnaissance, although they achieved their greatest fame through their bombing raids on England.

Britain in 1915. Although they did little damage, they caused anxiety and fear among much of the civilian population. For the first time in its history, Britain could no longer rely on the stretch of water that is the English Channel for protection.

BOMBER AIRCRAFT

The Germans followed up their airship raids with attacks by Gotha and Type R bomber aircraft. They were more effective than the airships, but their bomb loads were still too small to cause severe damage. However, they dented civilian morale and forced the British to devote vital resources to anti-aircraft defence. The British and French developed their own bomber aircraft, which had sufficient range to attack industrial targets in western Germany. Among the best of these was the British Handley Page 0/400, which could carry a bomb load of just under one tonne and had a range of 1,000 kilometres.

Bomb damage in the City of London from a 1915 zeppelin raid.

Air Attack On Britain

1915 19 January First ever air raid on Britain; two airships bomb Norfolk at night, killing four and wounding 15.

1915 13/14 October First major raid on London; 54 killed and 107 wounded.

1916 2/3 September Lieutenant W Leefe Robinson shoots down the first zeppelin in aerial combat over Britain. German airship losses begin to increase.

1917 25 May First Gotha bomber raid on Britain; 95 killed and 195 wounded in Folkestone, Kent.

1917 13 June Most successful raid of the war, as 14 German Gothas drop 72 bombs on London, leaving 162 people dead and a further 432 wounded.

1917 22 August Last daylight raid. German losses become too high to continue the campaign except under cover of darkness.

☞ ATTACK FROM THE AIR

◆ The Russian Ilya Muromets bomber was unveiled in January 1914. Designed by the helicopter pioneer Igor Sikorsky, this huge aircraft was the most advanced of its type.

◆ In support of the British offensive at the Battle of Loos in September 1915, bomber aircraft damaged five trains and severed railway lines behind the battlefield in 15 places.

◆ British air defences around London in April 1918 consisted of 266 anti-aircraft guns, 353 searchlights, 159 day-fighters and 123 night-fighters.

◆ The Royal Navy cruiser HMS *Furious* became the world's first aircraft carrier when it was converted to this role in 1917.

BREAKING THE DEADLOCK

The right combination of firepower and movement are normally vital to military success. On the Western Front in World War One, however, firepower dominated, making movement virtually impossible. All sides introduced new weapons and tactics to attempt to restore movement to the war.

POISON GAS

The first of the new weapons designed to break the trench deadlock was toxic gas, first used in a limited way by French troops against the Germans in August 1914. The first large-scale use of gas was by German forces on the Eastern Front in 1915 and, on the Western Front, at Ypres later that year.

British troops quickly followed the German lead, so that gas attacks became a regular part of any offensive. But gas could be countered by the use of gas masks, which greatly reduced casualties and, in the end, prevented any breakthrough by the attacking side.

THE ARRIVAL OF THE TANK

A more hopeful weapon was the tank, first used by the British at the Battle of the Somme in 1916. This new and cumbersome weapon was bulletproof and could

> *"Tank after tank, festooned with reserve petrol cans, caught fire, and in a few seconds they were red, glowing masses of metal, incinerators of their roasted crews. Out of 48 machines engaged, 32 were destroyed."*

A description of a failed French tank attack, caught in heavy German gunfire

GAS ON THE WESTERN FRONT

At Ypres in 1915, the Germans opened 500 canisters of pressurised chlorine gas and used the wind to blow the gas over to the Allied lines. The gas cloud caused panic among French colonial troops but the Allied line held and German forces failed to press home the advantage.

Chlorine attacked the lungs, making it incredibly difficult to breathe, causing great pain and fear and, sometimes, death. Fortunately, gas masks and box respirators minimised the effect of chlorine. The Germans introduced mustard gas in July 1917. This burnt the skin, lungs and eyes, effects that could be lessened by wearing a gas mask.

Gas masks

travel over heavy mud, crush barbed wire and cross enemy trenches.

The weakness of the tank lay in its slow speed and mechanical unreliability. The British and French continued to use tanks until the armistice in 1918 but they never proved to be the war-winning weapon that generals had hoped for.

In the end, no single weapon was able to break the stalemate caused by trench warfare. The Central Powers lost the war because they were slowly ground down by the superior economic and military strength of the Allies.

SUPREME TACTICS BUT LACK OF RESOURCES

In fact, the Germans developed the best tactics of the war. These tactics consisted of short but intense artillery bombardments followed by an assault by elite infantry called storm troops. They were specially trained to bypass enemy strong points in order to keep the attack moving, in the hope of cutting through the enemy's trench lines. In 1918 the Germans almost broke the Allied line, but they lacked sufficient resources to exploit their early success.

☛ GAS AND TANKS

◆ At least one million men became casualties as a result of poison gas. Although most survived, many of them suffered medical problems for the rest of their lives due to the effects of the gas on their lungs.

◆ The first British tanks to see combat on 15 September 1916 were operated by a crew of eight men, and were armed either with five machine-guns ("female") or two 6-pounder guns ("male"). They were capable of a top speed of only 5 km/h and frequently broke down.

◆ The Germans were not that impressed by tanks although they did use several captured British models. At the end of 1917 they produced a tank of their own, the A7V, but it was too heavy for cross-country travel.

◆ The British offensive at Amiens on 8 August 1918 was the biggest tank campaign of the war. On the first day of battle, 600 tanks were used.

A British Mark IV tank. This model entered service in August 1917; it served in the battles of Messines, Ypres and Cambrai.

THE GRIM LEGACY

In the years following the end of the war, soldiers and military thinkers looked back to see what lessons this terrible conflict might hold for the future.

MODERN TECHNOLOGY

World War One was the first major conflict to be fought by nations using the technology of the Industrial Revolution. The great advances in the defensive power of weapons had come as a surprise to the commanders on both sides. This was the main reason why mobile, offensive operations repeatedly failed with huge losses. But in spite of the heavy casualties – and the agony of trench warfare – there were signs that at the end of the war new weapons and equipment were pointing the way forwards to a more mobile form of warfare, which favoured the offensive.

A WEAPON FOR WINNING WARS

Great hopes had been pinned on tanks to break the trench stalemate, but they lacked both mobility and reliability. During the two decades that followed 1918, tank design improved enormously. By the outbreak of World War Two in 1939 not only were tanks highly mobile and mechanically reliable, they were well armoured and armed with both a main gun and machine guns. Tanks had developed into a war-winning weapon.

COMMUNICATION AND CONTROL

Perhaps the greatest problem facing commanders in World War One was their inability to keep control of their troops once battle had begun. This was largely solved by the development of light and reliable two-way radios, which came into service with most armies by 1939. Now small units and tanks could keep in permanent contact with their senior officers, being able to send back information from the battlefield and receive orders in return.

JFC FULLER

JFC FULLER (1878-1966) was a British soldier who eventually rose to the rank of Major General. He played an important role in the development of tank warfare during World War One. It was he who was first to see the potential of the tank as a highly mobile means of delivering firepower. His writings had considerable influence on German tank generals and their development of *Blitzkrieg* (lightning war) tactics during World War Two.

LOOKING AHEAD

◆ The founder of Germany's *Panzer* (tank) forces in the 1930s, General Heinz Guderian, had been a signals officer in World War One. He pioneered the use of signal equipment, such as radios, in armoured vehicles.

◆ During World War One, a tank advance of 10 kilometres was considered exceptional, but during the German invasion of France in 1940, some tank units travelled as far as 100 kilometres in a single day.

◆ The first large-scale air raid took place during the Spanish Civil War (1936-39). German air force units, helping the fascist forces under General Franco, attacked Guernica, deliberately destroying much of the city centre and killing many hundreds of civilians.

The ruins of Guernica in August 1937, after large-scale air raids.

SUPERIORITY IN THE SKIES

The other great development of World War One was military aviation. By 1918 aircraft had shown their potential as bombers, ground-attack aircraft and fighters. In the next two decades constant improvement would make air superiority an essential first step towards victory on the battlefield.

Not only did the war of 1914-18 make full use of the technology of the Industrial Revolution, it acted as a forcing ground for many new weapons and tactics that only reached their full potential in World War Two.

BOMBERS: THE DECISIVE WEAPON?

After World War One it was thought that fleets of bomber aircraft might be able to destroy the enemy's will to fight by attacking cities and other civilian targets. This theory was enormously influential during the 1930s and had a great effect on politicians. Although bombers did cause massive devastation during World War Two, civilian populations proved to be tougher than had been imagined and bombers proved to be vulnerable to fighter aircraft.

GLOSSARY

Allies The alliance of countries (primarily France, Russia, Britain and its colonies, Belgium, Italy, Portugal and the United States) who were at war with the Central Powers.

Armistice The agreement between Germany and the Allies that brought the war on the Western Front to an end on 11 November 1918.

Calibre The diameter or width of a gun barrel; the bigger the calibre the heavier the shell fired by the gun or howitzer.

Camouflage To attempt to conceal something from observation by an enemy, for example by painting it in such a way as to blend in with the surrounding terrain.

Central Powers The alliance of countries (Germany, Austria-Hungary, Turkey and Bulgaria) who were at war with the Allies.

Counter-battery fire Artillery fire against other guns, a vital part of any offensive.

Field gun A light artillery piece that fires a shrapnel or high-explosive shell at a low trajectory.

Grenade A small, hand-held steel container, filled with high explosive. It is designed to break up on detonation to cause maximum casualties through the blast of the high explosive and the metal fragments of the container.

Howitzer An artillery piece that fires a high-explosive shell at a high trajectory. It normally fires a more powerful shell than a gun.

Mobilisation The preparation of a country for all-out war, especially the organised call-up of civilians with military training to join the armed forces.

Mortar A steel tube used to fire high-explosive shells over short distances; used mainly by infantrymen.

No-man's-land The piece of land between the two opposing frontline trenches, typically ranging between 50 and 500 metres wide.

Reconnaissance The examination of enemy territory to gain information of their positions and intentions.

Sorties Combat missions flown by an aircraft.

Torpedo A long, cylindrical self-propelled weapon, containing an explosive charge, fired by warships and submarines to sink all types of ship.

U-boat A German submarine, from the German *Unterseeboot* (undersea boat).

WORLD WAR ONE CHRONOLOGY

1914
28 June Assassination of Archduke Francis Ferdinand in Sarajevo.

1-6 August War declared in Europe.

17 August Russian army invades East Prussia.

26-31 August Russians defeated by Germans at the Battle of Tannenberg.

5-10 September Germans defeated by Allies at the Battle of the Marne.

29 October Turkey enters the war on the side of the Central Powers.

30 October-24 November First Battle of Ypres: beginning of trench warfare on the Western Front.

1915
22 April-25 May Second Battle of Ypres: first use of poison gas on Western Front.

25 April Allies land at Gallipoli in an amphibious assault against Turkey.

23 May Italy enters the war on Allied side.

5 August Germans capture Warsaw.

6 October Serbia invaded by Central Powers.

23 October Beginning of Allied evacuation from Gallipoli.

1916
21 February-18 December Battle of Verdun: French defend the city from German attacks; heavy casualties on both sides.

31 May Battle of Jutland: an inconclusive action between British and German navies.

1 July-13 November Battle of the Somme: the Allies fail to break through German lines; heavy casualties on both sides.

15 September Tanks used for the first time by the British on the Somme.

1917
1 February Germany adopts unrestricted submarine warfare.

12 March Russian Revolution begins.

6 April United States declares war on Germany.

10 May Britain begins convoy system to safeguard merchant shipping.

7-8 June British capture Messines Ridge.

31 July-10 November Third Battle of Ypres (Passchendaele); British fail to break German lines.

7 November Bolsheviks seize power in Russia.

20 November British tanks break through at Cambrai but Germans soon restore the situation with a counter-attack.

1918
3 March Treaty of Brest-Litovsk signed between Bolshevik Russia and Central Powers; fighting effectively ceases on the Eastern Front.

21 March Opening of German Spring Offensive: Germans force the British to retreat but fail to break the Allied line.

8 August Battle of Amiens: successful British offensive, called by Germans the "black day of the German army".

5 October British break into main German defences on the Hindenburg Line.

6 October Germans request an armistice.

11 November Armistice comes into force at 11 am; the end of World War One.

INDEX